God's Finest©

Prayer & Devotional Book

By Tamekia Lee

ISBN 978-0-578-65017-3
Unless otherwise indicated, Scripture quotations identified are from the
Holy Bible, New King James Version ®. NKJV®. Copyright © 1982
by Thomas Nelson, Inc.
Unless otherwise indicated, all Scripture quotations are taken from the
Holy Bible, New Living Translation, copyright ©1996, 2004, 2007 by
Tyndale House Foundation. Used by permission of Tyndale House
Publishers, Inc. Carol Stream, Illinois 60188. All rights reserved.

This book recounts events in the life of Tamekia Lee according to the
author's recollection and perspective. While all stories are true, names
and some details have been excluded to protect the privacy of those
involved.

Editor, Dr. LaShonda Moorer
Cover design by Fallon A. McQueen | FMA Graphics
Front Cover Photography by Michael Carson | MCARSON
Photography Back Cover Photography by Michael Carson |
MCARSON Photography

Don't take no wooden nickels baby…

--My Granny

*This book is dedicated to God the Father, the Son,
and the Holy Spirit
Thank You for Your leadership, guidance and
power to transform!
I owe my FREEDOM, my ability to be
TRANSPARENT and all that I am to YOU...*

Contents

God's Finest Prayer & Devotional: Spending Time with God

Foreword

Introduction

Testimonials

I. Whose Attention Are You Seeking

II. Forgiveness – A Necessity

III. Patience – Before, During, and After the Storm

IV. Integrity – Our Silent Power Source

V. Speak No Evil

VI. Walking In Love

VII. Are You Willing to Plead

VIII. Grace – The Greatest Love Story

IX. You're In the Lineup

Foreword

If someone were to randomly ask you what changes needed to be made to make the world, your neighborhood, or your relationships better; would you have an answer? Truth be told, most of us would be amped and ready to provide a myriad of answers to these questions. But my question to you is, will the answers you provide to change the world involve you changing too? Or would it just be a list of ideas on how others need to change?

The famous Russian author Leo Tolstoy once said, "Everyone thinks of changing the world, but no one thinks of changing himself." From this statement we find a very poignant and often overlooked truth which is, if we want to see the world around us change, we must first change ourselves. And in order to change ourselves, we must be willing to allow the Holy Spirit to reveal and deal with the part of us that we so often try to hide.

This book, God's Finest Prayer & Devotional Vol. II, is a tool designed by the Holy Spirit to reveal and deal with the part of ourselves that we so often try to hide. Through my beautiful wife Tamekia's transparency and humility she gives you very real, insightful, and honest accounts of her intimate journey with the Holy Spirit as He has brought and continues to bring change and healing in her life. She reminds us that it's ok to be human while simultaneously inspiring us to pursue the possibilities that are available to us as we completely surrender to God and receive His extravagant love for us.

So, I encourage you as you read this book, make a commitment to apply the instructions and principles that are highlighted in each chapter. I encourage you to allow the Holy Spirit access to your heart so He can reveal and make the changes that need to be made. As you do this, you will see God not only change your life for the better, but you will also see Him transform your life and make it a light that shines brightly and inspires change in the world.

Pastor/ Loving Husband, Eric L. Lee, Sr.
River of Life Ministries
Birmingham, AL

Introduction

God's Finest Prayer & Devotional is a recollection of life accounts and prayers produced from years of listening to the Holy Spirit and allowing Him all rights to dive into the abyss of my past and pull up extremely painful memories and experiences that have shaped me into the woman I have become. It has been an exhilarating ride. He has taken my transparency and used it to help heal me and all who take part in a Saturday morning prayer call that He commissioned me to officially start in 2016.

God presented the idea in 2008. I immediately acted on it. I had beautiful professional business cards printed with the prayer call information. To my surprise, I was too chicken to pass them out. I remember walking through the mall wanting so badly to pass the cards out to everyone that passed by, but I was just too afraid! I did however pass out a few. The morning of the prayer call, the only person who called in was my sweet husband. He was so very encouraging and supportive. I went on with the prayer but felt very discouraged. I knew I had heard God say He wanted me to lead a prayer call, but I did not wait for instructions! It wasn't time yet. Why do we do that?

God told Abraham He was going to make him a father of many nations. Abraham and Sarah got so tired of waiting they took matters into their own hands. God told Moses he was going to lead His people out of Egypt. Moses took matters into his own hands instead of waiting on instructions from God and he ended up killing someone. There are many stories like these where people get a word from God and run with it before obtaining clear instructions. God offered me a glimpse of what my assignment would be 8 years before it would actually come to pass. Finally, in December 2015, after being pruned, nurtured and washed with Gods love, He gave me the ok. This time, I got real humble and created and printed off the instructions on these little 4x4 paper cut outs. With permission from my supervisor, I passed them out and posted an invite to Face Book and Instagram. The first official prayer call was hosted July 2016. I was both terrified and excited to see what God was about to do.

The first "official" prayer call hosted a total of 8 participants who called in at 7 a.m. on a bright Saturday morning. It lasted about 22 minutes as God had me speak and pray on loving our neighbors as we love ourselves. My supervisor shared how powerful and uplifting the call was to her and one of my coworkers also expressed her sincere thanks for the prayer.

God showed me the importance of waiting on His instructions and no matter how afraid I was to step out and do it, as long as I did it in faith and relied on Him, He would not leave me. Three years later, the prayer call is growing stronger than ever! I often wondered why God would have me write out my stories, testimonies and prayers. I now realize that He had a bigger plan, far bigger than I could have ever imagined.

I encourage anyone, please don't despise the day of small beginnings. God will use the purpose and plans He has for us to change the entire world one prayer at a time, one testimony at a time and one book at a time!!

Love,
The Author

Testimonials for God's Finest
Prayer & Devotional

Since 1ˢᵗ lady/cuzzo started the Saturday morning God's Finest prayer call, I have faithfully listened and commented on most of them. She truly has blessed me with her transparency and word of encouragement in overcoming and dealing with many of the same circumstances I have had to deal with in my personal life. This is such an honor and privilege since she asked me to share a testimonial to God's Fines. My encouragement to you is to keep using your God given talents and tools of encouragement in continuing to strive and reach out to others daily!

Blessings & Love,
*-**Amber C. Ellison***
Veteran Service Representative
Montgomery, AL

Tamekia's transparency in "God's Finest Prayer & Devotional" is proof that regardless of the mistakes we make in life, God can bestow on us a crown of beauty instead of ashes, the oil of gladness instead of mourning, and a garment of praise instead of a spirit of despair. (Isaiah 61:3NIV) This book is well written and encourages us to seek God's help in making everyday decisions as we strive to live God centered lives. God's Finest reveals the beauty of the author inside and out!

*-**Brenda Carter***
Mother-In-Love
COO, River of Life Ministries

I simply could NOT put this book down once I started reading. From the heartfelt foreward from her husband, Eric, to every "unfiltered" testimony that the author experienced. Everyone has a different way of experiencing God and how they came to know HIM! Mrs. Lee is telling her journey to God and it is so relatable and understanding through her written words. I truly love the format of the book! She gave her experience, how it relates to the Bible, and a prayer to pray for ALL that relates to that experience. It is an easy read with a deep dive of understanding our life choices but now giving up on yourself and becoming a BETTER YOU! I strongly recommend this book!!!

-Dr. LaShonda Moorer
Editor, God's Finest Prayer & Devotional Vol. II

Amazing. Mrs. Lee's book is so open and transparent. You can see how God has taught her through all of her choices and she freely, without judgment, shares it with us so we can learn and grow. Written simply in a no frills, straight to the point manner, this book blessed me. Her honest approach to God is so refreshing and teaches us to accept ourselves and learn from our mistakes without condemning ourselves. I left this book feeling loved and embraced by my Heavenly Daddy!

-Tonya Scott, Esq.
EEO Manager
Alabama Department of Labor

I.

Whose Attention

Are You Seeking?

John 5:44

How can you believe, when you receive glory from one another and you do not seek the glory that is from the one and only God?

Isaiah 2:22

Don't put your trust in mere humans. They are as frail as breath. What good are they?

As humans, we seek approval from our peers and loved ones…but how often do we seek God's approval? We must get to know God and His nature by first desiring His attention more than the attention of man. For years, I desperately wanted to be approved by people and sometimes even now I am tempted after being delivered. But when I was delivered, God taught me that I must first receive His love, accept myself and love myself. You can't effectively do anything, fulfill any calling, until you learn how to receive God's love. You do that by literally opening your mouth, saying and repeating, "I receive Your love God." Faith cometh by hearing. You must hear yourself say it over and over again so that it may sink in and become real to you. Once you receive His love, it will change you from the inside out.

You also receive His love by spending time with Him. When He wakes you up at 2 or 3 a.m. or an inconvenient time, get up. Don't turn on the TV or pull out your phone and get on social media. Go to your prayer closet or a quiet space and welcome the Holy Spirit to come and fellowship with you. Be willing to stay there until the Holy Spirit arrives! I'm a living witness, He will come. He will begin to teach you first how in Love He is with you and then He will draw you all the time. You can be doing human activities like watching TV or playing video games and you will feel a tug at your heart from the Holy Spirit to come and spend time with Him. Please don't ignore Him. Don't grieve Him by being disobedient, slothful, or idle. When you want prayers answered or a breakthrough, you want God to do it quickly right? So, let's honor Him in His role and be respectful. I remember the first time God showed me that I sought after the attention of man more than Him.

I was completely caught off guard as I was in church and the pastor was not preaching on this at all. LOL! It was one of those moments that God and I shared as He made an impression on my heart. That night, I went to Him, confessed and repented. It is so important to first acknowledge what God is showing you, confess it, repent and leave it with Him. Now, I am more conscious of my emotions and behavior when I need attention and go directly to God. Only God can truly fill that attention-seeking void.

If you are adequately spending time with God, pride flies right out of the window. You simply don't have time for any level of pride and when you are in His magnificent presence, you become vulnerable and recognize how very much you need the savior. When you spend quality time with God, He will fill you up to overflow. Don't get me wrong, we all desire attention, but you won't feel the need to act out or behave boisterously to seek that attention. If you notice, in the bible, the people that were closest to God, spent tons of time alone with Him on a regular basis.

One example was David, who was a man after God's own heart. He tended to His father's sheep, but while alone he learned how to pray, how to write beautiful poems to God such as the Book of Psalms. He was taught how to slay bears and kill lions becoming a protector of the sheep. This was the ultimate practice for killing Goliath and saving Israel from the Philistines. Jesus our Savior, is the ultimate example as He constantly got away to spend time in prayer. He was strengthened and reenergized, obtained instructions and became the savior of the world by dying and being raised from the dead. It was the greatest miracle of God.

Be willing to love God to the point of no return. Be completely sold out no matter the cost. Loving God to the point of no return means being willing to lose your life so that you can gain it. Face it, we need all of God and every single dose of His Word. The Word says, "'the wages of sin is death; which means, you have to actually work at sin to die, 'but the gift of God is eternal life." God freely gives life as a gift! He gives it to us and asks for it back because He knows we are incapable of managing our own lives successfully. Who better to manage our lives than our God, the absolute perfect supreme being who created us!

Let us pray.

Father in the Precious name of Jesus, we come before you in unity and agreement thanking you for life and life more abundantly. Thank you for every soul reading this, thank you for their obedience and faithfulness.

Thank you for being our creator, protector, manager and lover of our souls. Thank you for being our wonderful counselor, savior, healer, financial advisor, our peace, joy, and simply our Everything. There is none like You. We bless You and everything about You. We bless Your kingdom and everything and everyone in Your kingdom. Thank You for leaving the Holy Spirit with us as our guide and supreme leader. Thank You for helping us and showing us how to pray effectively.

Grace us to pray without ceasing just as continual prayer was offered up by the Saints for Peter. The chains fell off and You sent Your angel to rescue Him from Herod's Prison! Thank You for showing us that miracles can take place if we get in agreement and pray without ceasing.

Dad, we need You now like never before! Create in us a pure heart and renew the right spirit within us. Make every crooked place straight. Please don't leave one undone. Deliver us from ourselves and free us completely from people bondage, not to act out or become an island not needing anyone, but to be completely free to do your perfect will.

Thank You for drawing us to spend time with You. Thank You for the level of care and attention to pay to each of us. Thank you for making us feel like we are the most special of all of Your children.

Thank You for deeper levels of intimacy with You. We long for You.

We long to be in Your presence all the time. Help us to love You to the point of no return, unwilling to compromise for the approval of the world. You said greater works shall ye do! Put us in position to fulfill Your Word. We are on this earth for such a time as this. Don't let us sit idly by and not fulfill Your purpose and plans for our lives.

We desperately seek You. We seek Your approval, Your attention and not the attention of man. Thank You that we pay close attention to Your presence, Your whispers, Your impressions, Your chastisements, Your ways, Your thoughts, and Your awareness. Grace us to be willing to lose our lives so that we may find it in You. We ask You to quicken us, and we will call upon thy name. Develop in us the ability to pray without ceasing. Give us Your mindset. Deliver us oh God from the spirit of fear, the spirit of doubt, the spirit of unbelief, the spirit of rebellion, the spirit of defiance, the spirit of backbiting, pride, competition, jealousy, unforgiveness, poverty, stinginess, gluttony, and hatred. May the love of God be shed abroad in our hearts always and forever. Put a watch over our mouths lest we sin against You with our tongues. May the words of our mouths and the meditation of

our hearts be acceptable in thy sight in Jesus'
name, we pray, Amen.

II.

Forgiveness – A Necessity

Matthew 18:21-34

21 Then Peter came to him and asked, "Lord, how often should I forgive someone[a] who sins against me? Seven times?"

22 "No, not seven times," Jesus replied, "but seventy times seven![b]

23 "Therefore, the Kingdom of Heaven can be compared to a king who decided to bring his accounts up to date with servants who had borrowed money from him.

24 In the process, one of his debtors was brought in who owed him millions of dollars.[c]

25 He couldn't pay, so his master ordered that he be sold—along with his wife, his children, and everything he owned—to pay the debt.

26 "But the man fell down before his master and begged him, 'Please, be patient with me, and I will pay it all.'

27 Then his master was filled with pity for him, and he released him and forgave his debt.

28 "But when the man left the king, he went to a fellow servant who owed him a few thousand dollars [d] He grabbed him by the throat and demanded instant payment.

29 "His fellow servant fell down before him and begged for a little more time. 'Be patient with me, and I will pay it,' he pleaded.

30 But his creditor wouldn't wait. He had the man arrested and put in prison until the debt could be paid in full.

31 "When some of the other servants saw this, they were very upset. They went to the king and told him everything that had happened.
32 Then the king called in the man he had forgiven and said, 'You evil servant! I forgave you that tremendous debt because you pleaded with me.
33 Shouldn't you have mercy on your fellow servant, just as I had mercy on you?'
34 Then the angry king sent the man to prison to be tortured until he had paid his entire debt.

There is a level in Christ where walking in love and forgiveness comes second nature and vengeance is a nonfactor. Because forgiveness and walking in love is a decree from God and go hand in hand, you cannot have one without the other. It is ultimately impossible and the key to success.

Ezekiel 36:26 states, "I will take out your stony stubborn heart and give you a tender responsive heart.

To obtain this level, it takes spending invaluable time with God and allowing Him to remove all hurt, pain and residue of what others have done to you. If you are having problems in this area and find yourself holding grudges, wanting to retaliate, praying for someone's demise, etc., go back in the oven baby because you are not done!

What do I mean by that? Go back to the altar, go back to your prayer closet, prayer room or secret place and stay there until this is no longer an issue. Don't worry about how many times you go to the altar or your prayer closet. It is between you and God and no one else. You don't know what God is healing your heart from or how many layers He must go through. It's no one else's business how many times it takes for you to stay before the Lord to obtain your breakthrough. We have to allow God to set us free of people bondage.

Afterward, get every scripture, read every book on love and forgiveness or whatever issue it is until you are no longer reading or meditating on the Word, but you become the Word and the Word becomes you.

My husband Eric made an illustration, it's like you have been dipped in a solution like a cucumber and you are now a pickle. You are no longer recognizable. The transition is a whole lot smoother and easier if you completely submit yourself to God.

Let us pray.

Father in the precious name of Jesus, thank You for being so amazing. There is none like You in the all the earth. Your character is made from perfection. You cannot be controlled by man and Your love has no limit. Thank You for Your

Kingdom and everyone and everything in it. We bless Your Kingdom. Thank You that Your thoughts are not our thoughts and Your ways are not our ways. Forgive us for anything we have said or done toward You or Your people. Thank You for removing stony hearts and replacing them with tender responsive ones.

Completely subdue us with Your love, power and anointing to accomplish and fulfill the destiny for our lives. We acknowledge that without You, we are nothing, but with You we are everything. Grace us to forgive 7x70 times and forget what others have done to hurt us just as You forget and remember our sins no more. We pray that our hearts be filled with mercy. You said, vengeance is mine says the Lord, I will repay.

Remind us of Your Word. Write it on our hearts. Grace us to meditate and fall in love with Your Word. We seek You with our whole hearts and if there is any area not submitted, we offer it to You now.

We know it's wrong to hold grudges, so we offer every grudge, every mean thought and all bitterness to you. Grace us not to let go of You until You heal us. Melt it all with Your power and love oh God. Have Your way in every way and we bless adore and thank You. You are the lifter up of our heads. We know Your voice and the voice of a stranger we will not follow but flee from him. Grace us with the purest hearts, purest thoughts, purest actions, purest words and purest deeds.

Embody us with the answers and action to heal our families, our churches and the nations. We get in position, in our rightful places and pray to represent You with excellence. Thank you for doing exceedingly abundantly above all we could ever ask or imagine in our lives. Our confidence and hope lie in You! Save, sanctify and fill us and anyone not saved in Jesus' name we pray, Amen.

III.

Patience – Before, During and After the Storm

While on my lunch break, I decided to go to a grocery store in the area to pick up a few items. As I'm waiting in line, there is one other person ahead of me and the person being waited on. I think, this is a short line, I'll be out of here in no time. I can run my items home before returning to work and be back within the hour. The young lady being rung up by the cashier runs out of money, about $6.00. The cashier tells her that the card only has enough for $20 worth of groceries. The lady proceeds to argue with her that there is more money on the card. The cashier rings or attempts to run the card again, but the card zeros out after only a few items.

The lady says, "Well let me put something back." She and the cashier begin to look for an item to put back and the guy in front of me who only has one item to purchase starts to fidget and get impatient. After standing there and waiting for another 3-5 minutes, the lady finally decides what she wants to put back and the cashier attempts to finish checking her out. Now, the card for some reason would not work, and the cashier says, "I will have to ring the entire order again and proceeds to call a manager." By this time, I'm furious! The manager clears out the order and the cashier rings up the guy in front of me with the one item. He leaves and now it's just me standing there. So, they are ringing her items again, the cashier starts looking up a price item and says she will have to call the manager again.

Now I have already placed all my items on the counter. I start to throw my items back in the buggy and go to a different line! The cashier tells me she's sorry, but I didn't acknowledge her because I'm ticked. I go to another line, only to have to wait another 3-5 minutes to check out. By then I only have 12-15 minutes before having to be back at work. I purchased my items and ran to my car! Afterward, the Holy Spirit checked me and said, "That scenario could have been so different. You could have paid for her $6 item, showed her my love in the process, and been out of there in no time."

But instead, I allowed myself to get all worked up and impatient, so I wasn't thinking clearly. I was only thinking about getting back to work on time. I started to feel bad and repented. How many of us have been in similar situations?

How did you respond? If we would slow down and follow peace, these types of incidents could be avoided. God doesn't allow us to soak in the Word or sit in church and hear the Word and not give an opportunity to apply it.

The key is recognizing the opportunities and they are presented ALL the time. *Galatians 5:22-23* says, *"But the Holy Spirit produces this kind of fruit in our lives: love, joy, peace, patience, kindness, goodness, faithfulness, gentleness, and self-control."*

There is no law against these things! What if God were impatient with us the way we are impatient with each other? The young lady who was being checked out was clearly a Muslim as she was dressed in the attire and had an accent.

This would have been an awesome opportunity to show the love of God and even break down some stereo types of what she may have thought of African Americans, or women or Christians as I am all 3!

Also, we never know whose observing our behavior. We do know God is always watching and when we get it right, I believe our God is cheering us on saying, "That's my son! That's my daughter in whom I am well pleased!" Let's make Him proud!

Let us pray.

Father in the name of Jesus, Thank You for being the greatest Dad known to mankind. Thank You for every storm, every test, and opportunity we get to make You proud! Thank You for the love You have put in our hearts to love one another. We repent of any times we have failed to show Your love and kindness. Your Word says they know us by our love. Grace us to always follow peace and only use anger in constructive ways to bring about positive change.

Thank You that everything happens for a reason and all things work together for the good of them who love You and are called according to Your Word. Thank You for raising us up to be mighty men and women of God! Thank You for the progress You have made in us! Thank You that when You give Your test and we fail, You always provide another opportunity to get it right. Thank You that where the Spirit of the Lord is, there is liberty! And liberty is freedom!

Freedom to be everything You have called us to be in Christ Jesus. We surrender every day Holy Spirit. We surrender every area of our hearts to You oh God. We surrender our plans, our goals, our pleasures, our ambitions, our hurts, our futures, our pasts, our selfish ways, our egos, our sins, our pride, our physical appearances, our love, our lusts, our anger, our fears our health and all of our ways to You.

Thank You for helping us walk in the spirit so we will not fulfill the lust of the flesh. Grace us to clothe ourselves with tenderhearted mercy, kindness, humility, gentleness, and patience. Your Word says that hatred stirs up strife but love covers all offense. Grace us oh God to cover each other's offenses. Create in us the purest hearts, purest thoughts, purest actions and deeds.

Thank You for showing us that this race is not given to the swift nor the strong, but to those who endure to the end. Thank You for giving Your angels charge over us and may Your peace forever be the umpire of our hearts. In Jesus' Name we pray, Amen.

IV.

Integrity – Our Silent Power Source

One rainy morning, I was taking my 14- year-old son, EJ to the bus stop. There were several cars lined up with parents and kids sitting inside waiting on the bus. They were almost blocking the exit of the neighborhood on the corner. I parallel parked between two cars and pulled in front of a house out of the way. Once parked, my son's friend ran to get in the car with us as he was standing in the rain at the stop. For one split second, I thought, "I need to pull further out of the street and straighten my car up." I began to back up and all of a sudden, I hear a loud thud! Disclaimer: When you read on your mirrors that objects are closer than they appear, please believe it! I actually hit the lady's mailbox whose house I was parked in front of!

I screamed and as I'm reacting, the bus pulls up. I asked EJ to run to the door and knock and then run to the bus. A woman answered and I shouted out of the window, "I just hit your mailbox." After all the cars passed, I pulled in her driveway and gave her my name and number. By this time, its pouring rain, but I apologized about 100 times it seemed as I could not believe I had just run into this ladies' mailbox! After we exchanged information, I left and she texted me a few hours later with the quote. I almost passed out! It was a whopping $220 to replace the mailbox. I forgot, before she texted, she called and mentioned that she would contact the homeowner's association to find out the procedures and I agreed. I had no idea mailboxes were so expensive. She sent the quote to my phone and I called the company to provide my debit card information.

I remember thinking, God, I'm trying my best to save money and now I've created another $220 bill. Why Lord why? Nevertheless, I thanked God that I had the money. After the mailbox was replaced the next day, she texted me this message, "Mrs. Lee thank you for your integrity and taking care of this so quickly. Most people would have just driven off. I pray that God will richly bless you."

In short, it is always best to do what is right, even when it feels horrible. A couple of times I thought maybe I should ask her to obtain more than one quote or see if it could be repaired rather than re-placed, but homeowner associations have certain guidelines that have to be adhered to, so I didn't even bother asking, I just paid it. I encourage you, apply what you are learning in church and in the Word and make God proud by passing the tests. Remember, things could always be a lot worse.

Let us pray.

Father in the name of Jesus, Thank You for being our Lord and Savior Jesus! Thank You for loving us beyond our faults. Please forgive us for anything we've said or done to You or Your people. We release our faith to You and as David said, search our hearts, o God, and know our hearts; test us and know our anxious thoughts. Point out anything in us that offends You and lead us along the path of everlasting life. We desire to be completely and totally honest with You about everything. Don't let us hold out on You.

Thank You for every test because they strengthen our resolve. Thank You that we don't just sit in the pews at church every Sunday and soak up the Word, but don't apply it to our everyday lives. Your Word is alive and well and we bless You for leaving it here with us as a set of instructions to guide our everyday lives. Grace us to live the best quality of life possible.

Take our everyday routines and use them for Your glory. We want to be living, breathing clones of You. Thank You for allowing us to break out the box of others. We live by Your rules, not the traditions and approval of man.

Isaiah 2:22 says, *"Don't put your trust in mere humans; they are as frail as breath, what good are they.*

Thank You for giving us the courage and boldness to stand for what's right and not back down to the enemy knowing that He's more afraid of us than we are of him. We plead the blood of Jesus over every person, situation, ailment, distraction, failure and success. Our hope and faith are in You. Your Word says You're looking for someone to bless. Bless us. Here we are waiting for You. Your Word says how precious are Your thoughts about us, o God. They cannot be numbered. We can't even count them; they outnumber the grains of sand! How excellent is thy name in all the earth!

Empty us out of all anger, impatience, lack of integrity, instability, ungratefulness, complaining, stubbornness, rebellion, lack of compassion for our fellowman, wrong thinking and wrong behavior.

We draw close to You. If we don't love You the way we should, put Your love so deep in our hearts, that we will love You the way You desire and deserve to be loved. If we don't trust You the way that we should, please put Your trust so deep in our hearts, that we will trust You the way You deserve to be trusted.

Thank You for great attitudes during the tests. Thank You for blessing us with Your integrity. Thank You that we are Your ambassadors here on earth and we are so honored to serve at the pleasure of our God. In Jesus' Name we pray, Amen.

V.

Speak No Evil

James 4: 11-12, *says, "Do not speak evil against one another, brothers. The one who speaks against a brother or judges his brother, speaks evil against the law and judges the law. But if you judge the law, you are not a doer of the law but a judge. There is only one law giver and judge, he who is able to save and to destroy. But who are you to judge your neighbor?*

Proverbs 16:28, *says, "A troublemaker plants seeds of strife; gossip separates the best of friends.*

Proverbs 17:9 *Whoever covers an offense seeks love, but he who repeats a matter separates close friends.*

Ephesians 4:29 *Let no corrupting talk come out of your mouths, but only such as is good for building up, as it fits the occasion, that it may give grace to those who hear.*

James 3:8 *But no human being can tame the tongue. It is a restless evil, full of deadly poison.*

Proverbs 18:20 *Death and life are in the power of the tongue, and those who love it will eat its fruits.*

Growing up, I found myself gossiping and always very interested in what everyone else had going on. In other words, I was always in other people's business. If it was going on, I wanted to know and didn't want any details left out. LOL! This started when I was a tiny little girl. Once, I overheard my granny talking about my granddaddy to my mom.

She said, "I'm tired of him staying out all night and using up all my cologne!" I repeated every word I heard them say to my granddad. I also remember getting my behind whipped! It's astonishing how the Holy Spirit will bring up long forgotten memories. I was a talker and repeated everything I heard as a child. During my teenage years, I became wiser, and started to realize the damage this type of behavior caused.

Early on in my relationship with God, as I spent time with Him, I noticed my heart being changed from this vile talking gossiping spirit. He began to teach me how valuable I was to Him and how important it was for me to control my tongue. He would impress upon my heart that I could not share everything He showed or shared with me.

While at work several years ago, I noticed anytime I was around certain individuals, and they would be discussing someone in the form of work or business, it would always get personal and go south (they started speaking negatively about whoever they were discussing). My heart would grieve but I didn't know why. The Holy Spirit brought to my attention that is was the spirit of gossip and backbiting.

Now, what is gossip? The bible commentary says, "that gossip is making up or passing along false reports which was strictly forbidden by God. Gossip/rumors, slander, and false witnessing undermine families, strain relationships and even add chaos to the justice system. Yet we often pass on unverified information in the form of prayer request or news. Even if you don't initiate a lie, you become responsible if you pass it along."

I have even noticed about myself, if I hear someone gossiping and start to think judgmental thoughts about that person, I soon find myself talking "confidential," gossiping about them. It is so important to remove yourself from these types of

situations and pray that God will heal that person's heart of gossiping and backbiting. If not, you'll find yourself in a similar situation as the bible says, judge not lest ye be judged. And this keeps us humble, because we are no better than anyone else.

I have also noticed that even if I am around someone gossiping and don't say anything, but laugh or just listen, my heart gets grieved because being in the midst, participating by laughing sends the message that I condone it. Although we can't always prevent these kinds of conversations, we do have the power to remove ourselves or take authority over the spirit of gossip/backbiting and pray for those that are not healed of these issues.

Titus 2:7-8 *and you yourself must be an example to them by doing good works of every kind. Let everything* *you do reflect the integrity and seriousness of your teaching. Teach the truth so that your teaching can't be criticized. Then those who oppose us will be ashamed and have nothing bad to say about us.*

Living this way gives our lives a greater impact. As the old saying goes, don't do as I say, do as I do! These types of sins such as gossiping and backbiting only satisfies the flesh. Following what the flesh wants only leads to slavery.

Most people think freedom is the ability to do anything you want. But it only leads to self-gratification. You are no longer free, but a slave to what your body dictates. Thank God that Jesus has freed us from the desires and control of sin. Have you been released?

Let us pray.

Father in the name of Jesus, Thank You for this powerful lesson and every scripture written about gossiping and backbiting. Thank You for teaching us how powerful the tongue is. Thank You for allowing us to come together again in agreement with Your Word. Thank You for being an awesome God, powerful Savior, mind-regulator, judge and jury, heart-fixer, redeemer, Alpha and Omega, Catalyst, Creator and above all else a true friend. We repent of any gossip/slander or backbiting in the name of Jesus.

We realize this is a heart issue and ask that You would totally and completely heal our hearts of this sin. Even those of us that have been on the receiving end of malicious gossip and back biting, we pray that You would fill our hearts with so much love and forgiveness that we would always cover the offense.

We know that for us to truly represent You, we must learn to speak like you, think like You and operate the way You do. Thank You so much for showing us how to successfully handle difficult situations we find ourselves in. Thank You for giving us the courage and boldness to walk away and not participate in gossip and backbiting.

We surrender all pride in our hearts to You. We pray for the purest hearts, purest actions, purest thoughts and purest deeds. Thank You for the spirit of discernment and showing us how to watch out for those who strive to cause division with gossiping and backbiting. Grace us to fast and pray for those individuals, that they may be completely delivered and set free. Your Word says death and life lie in the power of the tongue. Deliver us from a loose tongue. Deliver us from a judgmental tongue. Deliver us from an acerbic tongue which is bitter. Deliver us from a grumbling tongue. Deliver us from a gossiping tongue.

Thank You for gracing us to walk in freedom with the evidence of a gracious tongue, a truthful tongue, and an encouraging tongue. Thank You that You bless us when people mock, persecute, lie and say all sorts of evil things about us because we follow You! Thank You for great rewards in heaven and blessing us here on earth. Grace us not to copy the behavior and customs of this world but transform us into a new person by changing the way we think. Grace us to never think more highly of ourselves than we should. Thank You that we measure ourselves by the faith You have given us.

Grace us to never take revenge. You said, "It is mine to avenge; I will repay," says the Lord. Instead, grace us to feed our enemies if they are hungry; give them something to drink, if they thirst. In doing this, we will heap burning coals of shame on their heads. Thank You for victory in that we will conquer evil with good! We present our bodies as a living sacrifice, holy and acceptable to You. In Jesus' name we pray, Amen.

VI.

Walking In Love

Ephesians 5:2

² And walk in love, as Christ also hath loved us, and hath given himself for us an offering and a sacrifice to God for a sweet smelling savour.

Walking in love requires giving up everything. Laying down our motives and desires just as Jesus did in the Garden of Gethsemane. He said in my translation, "If at all possible, take this cup from me, nevertheless thy will be done." He gave up His will in exchange for the throne! To sit at the right hand of the Father. Are you willing to give up everything?

Are you willing to lose your life in exchange to gain everything? Walking in love requires meekness. It's the power to retaliate, but the endurance to just chill and take it. Can you take injury and not retaliate? The answer is Yes. It is a part of your DNA. You are built for it. If you are in Christ, it's easier to endure. But while enduring, you are pouring out to God, releasing the toxins, such as pain, hurt and defenses that are caused by not being able to retaliate or respond the way your flesh wants to.

My husband and I were having major problems some years back. Our issues had escalated to the point that he was ready to call it quits. I will never forget those words, "I want a divorce." They stung my soul! There were days that I was in constant warfare and my heart actually hurt. I was bombarded with questions in my mind like, what will people think of me? Am I a failure? Why doesn't he love me? Is this how it will end? Am I this unlovable?

It was torture every day for months. I tried to get marriage counseling and could never get an appointment. I was laying in my daughter's room one day, and I heard the Holy Spirit say, "I am Your Wonderful Counselor!" I immediately jumped up and replied, "Ok, if You are my Wonderful Counselor, I will take You at Your Word! Meet me in the morning." I still cannot believe I told the Holy Spirit to meet me as if He had to do anything I requested. LOL!

The Holy Spirit woke me up at 3 a.m. Back then, I met Him in the living room. The prayer closet was much later. I poured my heart out while my hubby was in the other room snoring, sound asleep without a clue of my divine meetings. The Holy Spirit had me pray the Word. I literally prayed **Ephesians 1:16-23** and **Ephesians 3:14-21**. I inserted my husband's name and my name in the scripture and prayed it for hours over and over again. It brings back tears as I write this. That was one of the most painful seasons of my life. God told me not to retaliate or say anything if my husband said something hurtful to me. God said, "Walk in love and pray." And then, "Bring all the hurt, all the pain to me. Tell me everything he did and said to you. Release Your tears. Tears wash the soul of a man. Then let me tell you about yourself. Let me show you your part in all the drama. It's always two sides to every story. Now once you are ready to take responsibility for your part, I can heal you. Now you're ready to take some more. The more you can take, the weaker the enemy's hold on him will become.

The more you can admit your wrongdoing, and the evil part you played, the looser the grip of the enemy becomes. Are you willing? If you are willing to lay aside yourself, desires and vengeance, the reward is astounding. It is freedom in Christ and the restoration of your marriage which can change the entire trajectory of your future and future generations to come."

He had me use my authority in the spirit realm as a wife and break generational curses of divorce on both sides. I also got every scripture on love, read every book on love and forgiveness that I could find until I was no longer reading or meditating on it, but I became the Word and the Word became me. As this went on for about a 2-3 months, I begin to notice the change in both our attitudes toward each other.

The love was never lost, but the lack of respect and boundaries that were pushed had reached a breaking point.

God completely restored the marriage and healed our hearts toward each other. I have never been so grateful in my life. Are you willing to walk in love? Are you willing to be the bigger person and walk in meekness? He and I are a constant work in progress, but we are determined that our marriage and relationship will reflect the very nature of God. We are now more committed than ever.

Let us Pray.

Father in the name of Jesus, Thank You for Your awesome revelation knowledge. Thank You Daddy, for showing us how wonderful You are. Your character is made from perfection. You cannot be controlled by man and your love has no limit. Thank You for Your kingdom. We repent for anything we've done or said toward You or Your people. We release everything in our hearts to You that is hindering us from completely surrendering to You!

We yield our hearts, thoughts, actions and minds completely to You. Thank You that Your Word is a lamp unto our feet and a light unto our paths. Thank You for opening the eyes of our understanding. We delight ourselves in You and You alone. Strengthen us in meekness and being able to endure injury with patience and without resentment. Thank you that your thoughts are not our thoughts, your ways are not our ways. Grace us to be strong in You and know our boundaries in the earth. Grace us to use wisdom and not cross the boundaries of others in disrespectful ways.

Thank you for removing stony hearts and replacing them with tender responsive ones. Completely subdue us with your love, power and anointing to accomplish and fulfill the destiny for our lives. We acknowledge that without you we are nothing, but with you we are everything. Grace us to forgive 7x70 times and forget what others have done to hurt us just as You forget and remember our sins no more. We break every generational curse of divorce, infidelity, adultery, secrecy, rebellion and defiance. Show us our power and authority in the spirit and allow us to walk in it all the days of our lives. We seek you with our whole hearts and if there is any area not submitted, we offer it to you now.

Have your way in every way and we bless, adore and thank you. You are the lifter up of our heads, we know your voice and we always obey. Grace wives to be submissive, respectful, loyal and kind always. Grace husbands to be loving, loyal, dutiful and respectful always. Strengthen marriages and bind husbands and wives together as a 3-prong chain that cannot be easily broken. Prepare singles for their mates. Make us all whole and complete in You. Our confidence and hope lie in You! Embody us with the knowledge, the answers, and actions to heal this nation. We get in position in our rightful places and vow to represent you with excellence.

Thank you for doing exceedingly abundantly above all we could ever ask or think according to the power that worketh in us. Fill our cups to overflow. Thank You for preparing a table before us in the presence of our enemies. Thank You for the spirit of wisdom and revelation in the knowledge of our Lord and Savior Jesus Christ. Thank You that we are seated with Christ in the Heavenly realm. Save, sanctify, and fill us and anyone not saved in Jesus' Name we pray, Amen!

VII.

Are You Willing to Plead?

2 Corinthians 5: 18-21

18 And all of this is a gift from God, who brought us back to himself through Christ. And God has given us this task of reconciling people to him.
19 For God was in Christ, reconciling the world to himself, no longer counting people's sins against them. And he gave us this wonderful message of reconciliation.
20 So we are Christ's ambassadors; God is making his appeal through us. We speak for Christ when we plead, "Come back to God!"
21 For God made Christ, who never sinned, to be the offering for our sin,[a] so that we could be made right with God through Christ.

I remember being approached by a saint who witnessed to me. I was 16 years old working a part time job after school. She just simply came up to me and asked was I saved? I don't remember my response, but her words compelled me, and I went to one of her church bible studies and gave my life to Christ. Immediately, I knew something was different! God answered every prayer I prayed! I also remember getting into three car accidents on the same day as I thought I could go back to my old lifestyle. I didn't fully understand the commitment I had made, but I soon came to understand.   LOL!

God begin to clean me up from the inside out and it was amazing as I was a total wreck.

I was fornicating, cussing, drinking, lying, wanting to fit in so badly with my peers ect...so her approaching me couldn't have come at a better time. I think back and wonder, what if she hadn't because she was afraid, had something more important to do, or just plain didn't care. Where would I be right now? I am so very grateful that she took the time to witness to me.

Are you willing to plead for someone's life? In the scriptures, God has given us (Christians) the task of reconciling people to Him. We are Christ Ambassadors. God is making His appeal through us. We are speaking directly for God when we plead, come back to God! He's been waiting for you with open arms. So, remember when God compels you to witness to that person in the store, a friend, a family member ect...you are making an appeal on His behalf.

There have been times when the Holy Spirit would compel me to witness to someone and I would punk out because of fear of rejection. Afterward, I would feel this overwhelming grief in my heart for being disobedient. To combat this fear, I started meditating on the scripture, "God has not given me the spirit of fear, but of love, power and a sound mind. God is with me and I can do all things through Christ who strengthens me."

God also impressed on my heart that I should always remember the courage my coworker demonstrated by witnessing to me. What if she had been afraid? This subject is very dear to my heart as I realize now more than ever, in this dark world, we must allow our lights to shine, so others may walk out of darkness into His marvelous light.

Let us pray.

Father in the name of Jesus, we thank you for being our King, our Savior, our Dad. Thank You for being all things to us. Thank You for caring about all aspects of our lives. Thank You for being our wonderful counselor, judge, lawyer, defense, offense and advocate. We choose to remain in You. We surrender all our passions and desires to You.

Thank You for choosing us as Your ambassadors and if there is anyone reading this that is not save, we pray that the convicting power of the Holy Spirit arrest your heart and you give Jesus Christ full reign your lives. Create in us the purest hearts oh God.

Uproot every negative seed that's ever been planted in our hearts. Thank You for reminding us in Your Word that we have a grave responsibility to reach the world one person at a time by letting them know salvation is for them and once they become saved, old things are passed away. Thank You that their old lives cease to exist and they have been given a brand new life in You!

We break the power of fear, intimidation, selfishness and ignorance. Grace us to shake the dust off of our feet when people reject our witness. Guard our hearts oh God against the hand of the enemy.

Don't allow us to be deterred from witnessing when we are rejected. Greater is He who is in us than he who is in the world! Move by Your spirit in compelling us to bring others to Christ. In Jesus' name we pray, Amen!

VIII.

Grace – The Absolute Greatest

Love Story

Have you ever thought what if God hadn't saved me? What if forgiveness wasn't attainable? What if God who loves us so much, decided not to humble Himself, come down in the form of a man and make the greatest sacrifice ever known? If you've ever thought about any of these questions, it might be frightening! Years ago, I backslid and fell from grace, it was one of the scariest times in my life.

I was living with a man who wasn't my husband and I knew it was wrong to shack. I had never felt so distant from God. It literally felt like death and I remember the Holy Spirit telling me don't do it, come back to God. He loves you. As much as I wanted to get my life right, I felt like sin had such a tight grip on me and I just could not pull free.

Of course, the relationship was detrimental. He was manipulative, possessive, and extremely controlling. The relationship was verbally and physically abusive as well. It all starts out fun at first. You think you're in love and this one scratches every itch, but that's what sin does! It subtly lures us away from our very first love. And God, who is such a gentleman, will forewarn and speak to you gently, to get your attention, but after a while, He turns you over to sin.

One night the guy and I had gotten into a heated argument. He was out getting us something to eat and his cell phone but dialed me. I answered and sat there listening to him trying to talk to another girl and get her number. When he got back to my apartment, I had thrown all of his clothes outside.

My neighbor called the police and they escorted him away. As he was leaving, he called me a "broke b****" in front of the police. I was so embarrassed! He moved into my one-bedroom apartment with me and I'm the one who is broke?!

I finally got fed up and sick of living in sin. I got rid of him and ran back into the arms of God. I can never thank God enough for blessing me with a true man of God who loves me and treats me like a queen. Why did it take me going through all that chaos to see, that wasn't the lifestyle or life God had for me?

My initial questions were, what if God didn't offer forgiveness and grace? What if He didn't offer second, third or fourth chances? Where would some of us be? There is so much more to that story that will be later revealed. The point is, if it wasn't for the redemptive power and grace of God, who knows where I would be.

Ephesians 1:6 *says, "So we praise God for the glorious grace he has poured out on us who be- long to His dear son. He is so rich in kindness and grace that He purchased our freedom with the blood of His Son and forgave our sins.*

Ephesians 2:4-10 *But God who is rich in mercy, because of His great love with which He loved us, even when we were dead in trespasses, made us alive together with Christ (by grace you have been saved, and raised us up together, and made us sit together in the heavenly places in Christ Jesus, that in the ages to come He might show the exceeding riches of His grace in His kindness toward us in Christ Jesus. For by grace you have been saved through faith, and that not of yourselves; it is the gift of God, not of works lest anyone should boast. For we are His workmanship, created in Christ Jesus for good works, which God prepared beforehand that we should walk in them.*

Grace is an amazing gift from God! It's not a license to sin. Grace covers us because we are no longer under the law. We are now under grace. When we read the Word and come into the knowledge of what we should or shouldn't do, we simply obey the Word. If we don't obey, we must repent and confess our sins to Jesus. Don't allow them to fester and harden our hearts.

The Word says clearly as a man sows, that shall he reap. But, if we quickly confess our sins, God is so faithful to wash us clean. This is something we have to practice daily. When we mess up or veer too far to the right or left, God gently pulls us back, and in some cases "yanks" us back to His center. When we mess up, we must run to God! Don't run away from Him, run to Him! He's waiting with open arms!

Let us pray.

Father in the name of Jesus, Thank You first for loving us. Thank You for humbling Yourself, coming down to earth to take on the sins of the world. Thank You for sacrificing Your life, being raised from the dead and taking the keys to the Kingdom.

Thank You for all the pain and suffering You endured so that we might have the right to the tree of life. Thank You for leaving the Holy Spirit with us to guide us in all truth! Thank You for giving us the spirit of wisdom and revelation, the eyes of our understanding being enlightened that we may know what is the hope of Your calling and what is the exceeding greatness of Your Power to those who believe according to the working of Your mighty Power!

We thank You for saving grace, forgiveness, and Your love that covers a multitude. Thank You for Your faithfulness. We choose to completely let go and give You the reins! We pray that nothing or no one ever has a greater influence on us than You. We idolize and adore Your ways. We laugh with no fear of the future because we know our hope lies in You! We rest in Your presence and confess our sins quickly. We run to You in times of trouble and medicate ourselves with the Word of God.

We confess our sins to one another as You have commanded. We build each other up in the faith and refuse to be swayed by the enemy. Thank You that our strength lies in You. Our trust lies in You. Our faith lies in You. Thank You that You've chosen us to be the salt of the earth and our lights shine brightly so unbelievers and backsliders can see and find their way to You!

We build monuments in our hearts of all the blessings You have freely given, and we do not take You for granted. We repent of any ungratefulness in our hearts. We ask that You search every inch of our hearts and uproot anything that shouldn't be there. Thank you for gracing us with the greatest love story ever told featuring "us" Your children!

We walk in the power and authority You have given us, and we command that every chain be broken off of our lives. We pray for every person who has been physically, mentally or verbally abused. We ask that you send legions upon legions of Your angels to go forward in the spirit realm and fight and defeat the enemy on their behalf. We pray that You would keep us close to You not allowing the enemy to have any footholds in our lives. Peace be Still in the name of Jesus!

Thank You for Your grace and unmerited favor. We boast in our testimonies of how You heal our bodies, protect us from danger and the hand of the enemy. We adore how You, the creator of all, desire to spend one on one time with us. We praise You Dad and we give You all the glory. We humble ourselves before You and ask that You would please heal the land. We turn from our wicked ways and intently listen to Your instructions and guidance.

Thank You that we are not led by our flesh, but by our spirit. Bless us oh God! Bless us abundantly and we will forever give You all the honor and praise. Please help us stay focused on the Kingdom of God and not get distracted by the things and issues of this world. Heaven is Your throne and the earth is Your footstool. Who could possibly be afraid with a God of this magnitude! Thank You with all of our hearts. We long to fellowship and know You more intimately. In Jesus' name, we pray, Amen!

IX.

You're In The Lineup!

Years ago, I was sitting in a hair salon waiting to be seen and I overheard two other young ladies talking. One of them, I knew well, the other one I didn't. They both had attended college together and had recently gotten married. They were in marital bliss, laughing and bragging about how awesome their lives were.

I was quietly listening and the young lady that I knew well asked me was I married or dating anyone significant. I replied, "Do you know what's his face?" I knew they had gone to high school together, but I wasn't sure if they knew each other.

She rolled her eyes when I mentioned his name with disgust and disapproval. I said, "Yeah, my friend introduced us, and we've been going out." She turned back to the other young lady and continued talking to her as if I wasn't there. For some reason, I started feeling depressed and defeated.

At that time, I was a 24-year old backslider who had a kid out of wedlock just sifting through life trying to find my way. I remember thinking, "God have you forgotten about me?" I left the salon and completely forgot the ordeal.

Fast forward, a couple of years later, I rededicated my life to Christ, got rid of the joker that my friend introduced me to and a few others and started spending tons of time with God. Back then, I remember unplugging my phone and trying to get as close to Jesus as possible. I put God and my baby first. It was one of the most freeing times of my life. I was no longer trying to fill a void in my heart that only God could fill. I was no longer making decisions about my life without getting God's perspective first.

Then I met my incredible husband. We dated, got married and had our first kid. He then got promoted from youth pastor to co-pastor just 2 years after being married. Now, I am a co-first lady of a megachurch and the young lady that I didn't know who was sitting in that same hair salon laughing and in marital bliss is attending the annex my husband co-pastors! I had completely forgotten that ordeal until God brought it to my remembrance.

God, along with time had prepared me and He reminded me that every season in my life was a season of preparation. Preparation was taking place even when I was in a backslidden state.

God doesn't waste anything or any situation. He allowed me to hit rock bottom, so I only had Him to depend on. In the story of Joseph, he was sold by his brothers into slavery, thrown into prison and left forgotten a few times but all the while God was removing debris in his life such as showiness, bragging, self-sufficiency and adding total dependency on God. I know he had to have gotten frustrated at times, but he maintained faith in His God and when the time was conducive, he was made

2nd in command which positioned him to help his family, the same ones who sold him into slavery.

No worries. Don't fret. You've been left behind by God for a reason. You are in the lineup! You shall reap if you faint not.

Let us pray!

Father in the name of Jesus, Thank You that You are the lifter up of our heads. The earth is the Lords and the fullness thereof. You shine Your sweet glory on us as we are Your prized possessions. We thank You and repent if we have been impatient, fretful, and worriers of our current season.

We thank You that as we remain in You and You in us, we shall ask what we will and it shall be given. Grace us not to ask amiss. Thank You that You are with us and Your seeds have taken root in our hearts to love our enemies and be good to them who hate us, to forgive quickly.

Grace us to have mercy on others when they refuse to have mercy on us. We are Your seed oh God and we reflect Your glory. Thank You for showing us our infinite worth! Thank You that we are so thankful while currently in the lineup. Never losing sight of what You've already done! Thank You that the eyes of our understanding are being enlightened. We revel in Your faithfulness. We cheer You on and stand firm in our commitment to You! Thank You for doing exceedingly abundantly above all we could ever ask according to the power that worketh in us.

We ask that You would give supernatural strength to all of us that fill weak and tired of the ins and outs of day to day living, not feeling like we are progressing, but God shows us that we are in the lineup.

Thank You for blessing us with great attitudes while You are completing the work in our hearts. You are paving the way in our lives. You are removing all debris in our hearts making us whole and complete. Settle in our hearts what you have already done for us, how you have blessed us and remind us of what you have brought us out of.

You said to have faith of a mustard seed. A mustard seed is the smallest seed but has the ability to multiply rapidly. Multiply our faith. Feed and wash us with Your Word until we want no more. Your Word says, "And Peter was filled with the Holy Spirit!" Fill us oh God to overflow and give us opportunities to release what You have filled us with. Give us to release it without hesitation, without fear or dismay. We know Your voice and we always obey what You tell us is our meditation. In Jesus' Name, we pray, Amen.

Notes

Notes

Notes